My First Book of
Christmas

 Charlotte Guillain

Illustrated by Anna Jones

A & C BLACK • LONDON

Published 2012 by A&C Black,
Bloomsbury Publishing Plc
50 Bedford Square, London, WC1B 3DP
www.acblack.com
www.bloomsbury.com

ISBN 978 1 4081 8036 5

Printed in China by C&C Offset Printing Co.

This book is produced using paper that is made from wood grown
in managed, sustainable forests. It is natural, renewable and
recyclable. The logging and manufacturing processes conform
to the environmental regulations of the country of origin.

To see our full range of titles
visit www.acblack.com

1 3 5 7 9 10 8 6 4 2

Contents

Do you celebrate Christmas?

Angels

Mary

Joseph

Jesus

Do you know how Christmas started? Christians remember the birth of Jesus at Christmas. Many children act in nativity plays to retell this story.

Three Kings

Shepherds

Christmas is an exciting time of year! There are so many things to see and do. Are you ready to find out about all the things that happen at Christmas?

Read the clues on each 'What could it be?' page and then turn the page to find out the answer.

I can see something hanging on the wall. There's a picture on it covered in little squares with numbers on them. Someone is opening a square with the number one on it.

What could it be?

It's an Advent calendar!

Advent calendars count the days in December up to Christmas Eve on the 24th of December. 'Advent' means 'coming' and is the four weeks before Christmas. Inside each window on the calendar there's a picture or a piece of chocolate!

I can see some small figures. There are animals inside a building. A star is shining over the building.

What could it be?

It's a nativity scene!

A nativity scene shows the stable where Jesus was born. His parents, Mary and Joseph, and angels are there. Some shepherds and three wise men have come to visit the baby Jesus. They found the stable by following the star.

An **envelope** has come
through the letterbox.
When I open it I can see
a picture of a robin.
Glitter falls out as
I look inside!

What could it be?

The Jenkins Family
46 Florence Street
Hilltop village
East Lindon

It's a Christmas card!

People have been sending
each other **Christmas cards**
for over 150 years. Many people
send cards to their family and friends
to wish them a merry Christmas and
a happy new year. Today some people
send Ecards to each other using Email.

I'm outside a shop looking up at the dark sky. Bright light is shining down the street. Lots of people have come out to look and do their shopping.

What could it be?

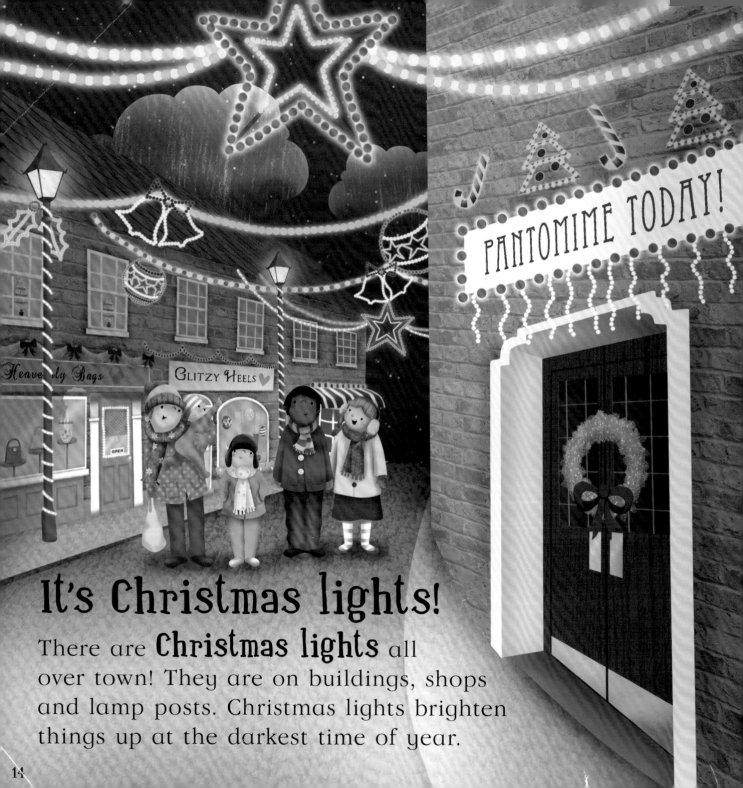

It's Christmas lights!

There are **Christmas lights** all over town! They are on buildings, shops and lamp posts. Christmas lights brighten things up at the darkest time of year.

I'm inside a theatre with lots of other people. On the brightly lit stage someone in a colourful costume is singing. The audience is shouting loudly.

It's a pantomime!

A pantomime is a special play that people watch at Christmas. There are lots of songs and jokes and the audience often joins in. Sometimes there are two people dressed up as a horse or a cow!

There is a sound outside my house. I go to the door and see people standing outside in the cold. They are all singing and looking very jolly.

What could they be?

They're carol singers!

Lots of people enjoy singing **carols** at Christmas. Many carols are hundreds of years old. People sing carols at church and out in the streets to celebrate Christmas.

I can see a circle of shiny green leaves.
The edges of the leaves are prickly.
There are bright red berries
among the leaves.

What could it be?

It's a holly wreath!

Many people make decorations using **holly** at Christmas. Its green leaves and red berries are special Christmas colours. Evergreen plants like holly remind people that spring and new life will soon be here.

I can see a sprig of green leaves hanging from the ceiling! There are white berries among the leaves.

What could it be?

It's mistletoe!

People have decorated houses with mistletoe for centuries. Many people hang mistletoe from the ceiling. It is traditional to kiss someone if you meet them under the **mistletoe!**

I can see the branches of a tree. They are covered in green needles. There is a lovely smell of pine in the air.

what could it be?

It's a Christmas tree!

The tradition of putting up a **Christmas tree** started in Germany. The evergreen tree decorated with lights celebrates Jesus's birth. Christmas trees became popular in Britain in Victorian times.

I can see colourful paper and shiny objects. Some are hanging from the branches of the Christmas tree. Others are on the walls and ceiling!

What could they be?

They're decorations!

People like to put up lots of **decorations** at Christmas. Tree decorations include baubles, gingerbread and chocolate. People cover their homes with paper chains and shiny tinsel.

There is something shiny being put on the Christmas tree. It's a golden colour and has five points. It's right at the top of the tree.

What could it be?

It's a star!

People put a **star** at the top of their Christmas tree to remember the star over the stable when Jesus was born. Some people put an angel or a fairy on top instead.

I can see something hanging at the end of the bed. It's red and made of wool. It's full of little presents and sweets.

What could it be?

It's a stocking!

Children hang out **stockings** on Christmas Eve for Father Christmas to fill with presents. In some countries, such as Spain and Italy, children put out shoes to be filled with presents.

I can see a person in warm red clothes. He's wearing big black boots and a red hat. He's carrying a huge sack on his back.

Who could it be?

It's Father Christmas!

Father Christmas is also called Santa Claus. He lives in the North Pole and makes all the toys for Christmas with the help of his elves. On Christmas Eve many children put out stockings for Father Christmas to fill with presents.

I can see a large animal with thick, light brown fur. Something is sticking up on top of its head like branches.

What could it be?

It's a reindeer!

Reindeer live in very cold northern countries and in the Arctic. They have large antlers on their heads and pull Father Christmas's sleigh on Christmas Eve. The most famous one is Rudolph who leads the way with his red nose.

I can see something wrapped in colourful paper. There is a ribbon round the outside and a label with someone's name on it.

What could it be?

To Ned........
From Grandad x

It's a Christmas present!

Most children think **presents** are the best thing about Christmas! The tradition of giving presents comes from the Christian idea that Jesus was a gift to the world. Christmas presents also represent the gifts of gold, frankincense and myrrh that the three wise men gave to Jesus.

I can see something wrapped in shiny paper. It's a tube shape that looks a bit like a big sweet. When I pull it there's a loud **BANG!**

What could it be?

It's a Christmas cracker!

Lots of people have **Christmas crackers** on Christmas day. Two people pull a cracker, which bangs when it splits open. Inside there is a paper hat, a joke and a small toy or gift.

Something is cooking in the hot oven.
It's golden brown and smells delicious.

What could it be?

It's a turkey!

Many people eat roast **turkey** for their Christmas dinner. Other people eat roast goose or chicken. A big turkey can feed a lot of people on Christmas day. Many people have cranberry sauce with it.

There is something round and fruity sitting on a plate. There's a piece of holly on top of it. Someone lights a match and there is a blue flame all over it!

What could it be?

It's Christmas pudding!

Christmas pudding, or plum pudding, has been made for hundreds of years. It's made with dried fruits, spices, nuts and sugar and cooked for a long time. Some people hide coins inside the pudding. If you find a coin in your slice of pudding it's good luck!

I can see something made of pastry. It smells sweet and spicy. When I bite into it, there's a delicious fruity filling.

What could it be?

It's a mince pie!

Mince pies are sweet pastries today but they used to be filled with meat! Now the filling is still called mincemeat but it's made of dried fruits and spices. Some mince pies have a pastry star on top to remember the star over the stable when Jesus was born.

Someone is snoring in his armchair. He's wearing slippers and a paper hat has fallen over his eyes. The cat has curled up at his feet.

Who can it be?

It's grandad!

All the presents are open and Christmas dinner is over. Everyone has had a busy day and **grandad** has fallen asleep by the fire. All over the world Christmas is nearly over . . . until next year!

 # Christmas quiz

Now you have read this book, can you answer these questions about Christmas?

1 What story do children remember when they perform in nativity plays?

2 What is Advent?

3 How long have people been sending Christmas cards?

4 What sort of special play do many people watch at Christmas time?

5 What happens if you meet someone underneath a decoration made of mistletoe?

6 Why do people put a star on top of their Christmas tree?

7 What do children in Spain and Italy put out for Father Christmas to fill with presents?

8 Where in the world do reindeer live?

9 What gifts did the three wise men give to Jesus?

10 What do you get if you find a coin inside your slice of Christmas pudding?